Contents

Safety at school

To stay safe at school there are a few things you should watch out for.

5

Keep tidy

You could trip over the toys in this classroom.

What could you do to make it safer?

Tidy up!

Pushing and shoving

What are these children doing?

What might happen to Lorraine if Jenny pushes her?

Running

Running inside might cause an accident.

Right

13

Say NO to strangers

If someone you don't know offers you some sweets in the playground, the safest thing to do is to tell your teacher.

Be careful with sharp things

Scissors cut paper
but they could cut
you too.

17

Fire alarm

If you hear the fire alarm ringing, what should you do?

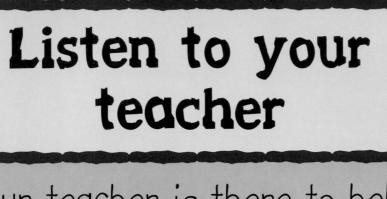

Listen to your teacher

Your teacher is there to help you stay safe.

Always do what your teacher tells you.

21

Index

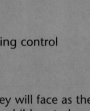

The end

Notes for adults

Stay Safe! supports young children's knowledge and understanding of the world around them. The four books will help children to connect safely with the ever-expanding world in which they find themselves. The following Early Learning Goals are relevant to this series:
• move with confidence, imagination and in safety
• move with control and co-ordination
• show awareness of space, of themselves and of others
• use a range of small and large equipment
• handle tools, objects, construction and malleable materials safely and with increasing control
• understand what is right, what is wrong, and why
• dress and undress independently and manage their own personal hygiene.

The *Stay Safe!* series will help children to think more about the potential dangers they will face as they grow up. Discussion can be focused on what makes an activity safe or unsafe allowing the children to learn how to protect themselves from harm. The books can be used to help children understand how their own behaviour can make a difference to their safety.

At school will help children extend their vocabulary, as they will hear new words such as *safety, classroom, pushing, shoving, accident, properly, strangers, teacher, careful, scissors* and *alarm*.

Follow-up activities
• Place items over half the floor area and leave the rest of the room tidy. Ask which is the safest place and why. Take this opportunity to tidy up the floor together, explaining where things go and why they are put there.
• Discuss issues of personal safety and respect for each other in the classroom and playground.